Turner's Water Colours At Farnley

J. M. W. Turner, A. J. Finberg

Alpha Editions

This edition published in 2024

ISBN : 9789362513465

Design and Setting By
Alpha Editions
www.alphaedis.com
Email - info@alphaedis.com

As per information held with us this book is in Public Domain.
This book is a reproduction of an important historical work. Alpha Editions uses the best technology to reproduce historical work in the same manner it was first published to preserve its original nature. Any marks or number seen are left intentionally to preserve its true form.

TURNER'S WATER-COLOURS AT FARNLEY HALL

TURNER'S PERSONAL RELATIONS WITH MR. W. FAWKE

IT is not known for certain exactly when or how Turner became acquainted with Mr. Walter Ramsden Hawksworth Fawkes of Farnley Hall. Several biographers say that Turner first met Mr. Fawkes about 1802, when the artist was in Yorkshire making drawings for one of the series of topographical works dealing with parts of Yorkshire which Dr. Whitaker, the vicar of Whalley, prepared and published. But Whitaker's "History of the Parish of Whalley," which was published about this date, contains no reference to Farnley, and deals with a part of Yorkshire and Lancashire at some distance from Farnley. The only book of Dr. Whitaker which contains any illustrations connected with Farnley Hall is the "Loidis and Elmete," published in 1816, and we know that Turner had become intimate with Mr. Fawkes some years before this date.

The first certain piece of evidence connecting Mr. Fawkes with Turner is contained in some of the sketch-books used by the artist during his first tour in Switzerland in the year 1802. Mr. Fawkes's name is not mentioned in full, but a capital "F" is written in ink on the margin or back of several of the drawings. I take this to mean that a patron whose name began with "F" had looked through Turner's sketch-books at some time after his return to London, and had selected certain subjects to be carried out from sketches thus marked. That this patron was Mr. Fawkes is established by the drawing made at Chamounix, which is inscribed in Turner's handwriting *"Mer de Glace, avec le Cabin de Blair"* (page 22 of the "St. Gothard and Mont Blanc" Sketch-Book in the National Gallery). The finished water-colour now in the Farnley Hall Collection, entitled *Blair's Hut on the Montanvert and Mer de Glace*, is simply an amplification of this sketch. Other subjects in these sketch-books which Turner carried out for Mr. Fawkes are *Bonneville, Sallanches, The Falls of the Reichenbach, The Valley of Chamounix, The Fall of the Staubbach, The Lake of Lucerne from Flüelen, The Lake of Brienz with the Ruins of the Castle of Ringgenberg,* and *Grenoble.*

The first point of connection between Mr. Fawkes and Turner thus seems to have been the scenery of Switzerland and not that of Yorkshire. In a description I have seen of Farnley Hall and its treasures, written soon after it came into the possession of Mr. Walter Fawkes, the only pictures mentioned are a series of "romantic landscapes in Switzerland and Italy, admirably executed by Warwick and Smith." The "Warwick and Smith" of this description is probably a misprint for "Warwick Smith," the name by which

John Smith, one of the earlier English water-colour painters, was generally known. This series of Smith's water-colours is still preserved in one of the lumber rooms at Farnley Hall. The drawings represent generally the same subjects as those which Turner treated. Smith's drawings are nearly all in monochrome, and, though they are not without merit, they look very dull and old-fashioned when compared with the Turners. It seems to me, therefore, extremely probable that Mr. Fawkes was first attracted to Turner as the rising young artist of his day, who was doing the same kind of work as Warwick Smith had done, but who was doing it with much more imagination, vigour, and artistic skill. If this surmise be correct, Turner made his first appearance at Farnley Hall as the successor and transplanter of Warwick Smith. His artistic function was to replace Smith's rather dull and laboured transcripts with his own brilliant and imaginative drawings.

The earliest of Turner's works in the Farnley Hall Collection is that of *The Mer de Glace, Chamounix*. This is probably the drawing exhibited at the Royal Academy in 1803, under the title "*Glacier and Source of the Arveron going up to the Mer de Glace, in the Valley of Chamouni*." Mr. Fawkes may have seen the drawing in the exhibition and bought it there or afterwards in the artist's studio. In a small pocket-book of Turner, apparently in use about the year 1804, there is a note that Mr. Fawkes had bought three water-colours for fifty guineas each. These are described by the artist as *Great Devil's Bridge Causeway, Upper Fall of Riquenbach* and *Mt. Blanc from St. Martin*. The first two subjects are still at Farnley, the third is probably the *Mt. Blanc from the Val d'Aosta* which passed from the Farnley Collection before the present owner came into possession. It was lent by Sir Donald Currie to the exhibition of "Old Masters" at the Royal Academy in 1906.

An earlier entry in the same pocket-book is the record of a commission for a small oil picture of *The Bowland, Lancashire*, to be painted for Mr. Lister Parker. Mr. Parker was a neighbour of Mr. Fawkes, and that he was also an intimate friend is proved by the inscription on the back of a fine miniature of Napoleon Bonaparte, which is still preserved at Farnley Hall. This inscription states that the miniature was bought in Paris in 1802, and presented to Mr. Fawkes in the same year by his sincere friend Mr. Lister Parker. So it is probable that Mr. Fawkes may have heard Turner's work talked about by his Yorkshire friends some time before he bought any of the artist's drawings, and it is quite possible that he may have made Turner's personal acquaintance through the intermediacy of those friends.

The next mention of Mr. Fawkes's name in the Turner sketch-books occurs in connection with the large mezzotint of Turner's oil painting of *The Shipwreck* (now in the National Gallery), which the engraver, Charles Turner, executed and published in 1806-1807. The name of "Fawkes" appears fifth in the list of subscribers to this plate, the first four names being the "Wells

Family," Sir William Beechey, Mr. Swinburne, and Mr. Henderson. Mr. Lister Parker's name appears lower down in the list.

It was probably in London that Mr. Fawkes first met Turner, and the two men had very likely known each other for some time before Turner was induced to pay a visit to his friend's home in Yorkshire. The first clear piece of evidence of Turner being at Farnley is in connection with Mr. Hawksworth Fawkes's story of the origin of Turner's large oil painting (now in the National Gallery) of *Hannibal crossing the Alps*. This picture was exhibited at the Royal Academy in 1812, so the incident described in the following words by Mr. Hawksworth Fawkes—he was a boy at the time—must have taken place in 1810 or 1811: "One stormy day at Farnley Turner called to me loudly from the doorway, 'Hawkey! Hawkey! come here! come here! look at this thunderstorm. Isn't it grand?—isn't it wonderful?—isn't it sublime?' All this time he was making notes of its form and colour on the back of a letter. I proposed some better drawing-block, but he said it did very well. He was absorbed; he was entranced. There was the storm rolling and sweeping and shafting out its lightning over the Yorkshire hills. Presently the storm passed, and he finished.

'There! Hawkey,' said he, 'in two years you will see this again, and call it *Hannibal crossing the Alps*.'"

The earliest oil painting of Turner's that Mr. Fawkes bought was the beautiful sea-piece sometimes called *The Pilot Boat*, and sometimes *Red Cap*. This was exhibited, in the "one-man show" Turner held in his studio in 1809, under the title *Shoeburyness Fishermen hailing a Whitstable Hoy*. There is a pen-and-ink sketch of this picture inside the cover of the "Greenwich Sketch-Book" (cII, Turner Bequest), and on the fly-leaf appears the following record of drawings made, or to be made, for Mr. Fawkes:—

"4	Proofs of 'Liber Studiorum.'	
	Mill. Sketch.	Per Contra
1	Mill. Drawing.	C. Draft.
2	Bardon Tower.	Feb. 20. £100."
3	Farnley.	
4	Gordale.	
5	Rocks.	
7	Weathercote.	
8	Geneva.	

9	Bolton.	
10	Thun."	

And on page 52 of the same book there occurs the following still longer list:—

"Mill, finished.
Mill, sketch.
Bardon Tower.
Armutic Rock.
Farnley.
Gordale.
*The Strid.
Weathercote.
*Bolton Abbey, West.
Lac de Thun.
Lac de Geneve.
Ps. V. (*Probably the Swiss waterfall known as the "Pisse Vache."*)
*Bonneville.
Ingleboro.
Bolton.
Blair's Hut.
Stourback. (*Evidently the Fall of the Staubbach.*)
Mt. Blanc.
Vevey.
Grundelwald.
*Brintz." (*The Lake of Brienz.*)

* These are among the drawings selected for reproduction in the present publication.

These entries were made, I am inclined to think, either in the year 1809 or 1810. It is easy to identify most of the drawings referred to in this list, in spite of Turner's rather arbitrary spelling. I can, however, find no trace of the drawings described as *Armutic Rock* and *Gordale*, and I have never seen either the sketch or the finished drawing of the *Mill*. I am not even sure what mill it can have been. It was probably the one at Otley, which stands close to the lodge at the entrance to the Farnley Hall grounds. A *View of Otley Mills, with the River Wharfe and Mill Weir*, said to have been presented by Mr. Fawkes to the family of its owner, was sold at Christie's in June 1890, and bought by the famous French dealer, M. Sedelmeyer. It was probably this drawing to which Mr. Fawkes refers in the only fragment of a letter in his handwriting which I have been able to discover among the Turner papers in the National Gallery. The body of the letter has been destroyed, but the last two paragraphs and the signature remain. This fragment says:—

"By to-morrow's coach I shall send you a box containing two pheasants, a brace of partridges, and a hare—which I trust you will receive safe and good. We have tormented the poor animals very much lately and now we must give them a holiday.

"Remember the Wharfdales—everybody is delighted with your Mill. I sit for a long time before it every day.

"Ever very truly yrs.,
W. FAWKES."

The "Wharfdales" are evidently the series of drawings of Wharfedale scenery which Turner had in hand for Mr. Fawkes. The allusions to the drawing of the *Mill* give us a clue to the real bond of union between the two men, viz., the patron's sincere and unaffected delight in the artist's work.

Mr. Fawkes's liberality as a buyer of Turner's work is demonstrated by some financial jottings made in one of his sketch-books (CXXII, Turner Bequest), during the years 1809 and 1810. In one of these statements of Turner's assets Mr. Fawkes is debited with £500, in the other he is entered as the artist's debtor to the extent of £1,000.

In 1811 Turner threw himself enthusiastically into the project of writing a long poem extolling the beauties and recounting the history of all the chief places of interest on the southern coast of England. The poem was to be illustrated by a series of engravings to be made from water-colours specially painted by the artist for the work. The poem was never completed, but Turner seems to have spent the greater part of the summer of 1811 wandering along the coast from Christchurch, in Hampshire, to Land's End, in Cornwall, diligently making hundreds of wonderfully delicate and accurate sketches, and with equal diligence, and perhaps just as much enjoyment to himself, grinding out even a greater number of lame and halting lines of the most indifferent verse. He returned along the northern sides of Cornwall, Devon and Somerset, sketching and rhapsodizing upon the whole coast from

Penzance to the Mendip Hills. This work and play must have kept him too busy to visit Farnley that year.

Turner was back in Devonshire and Cornwall in 1813, but I believe he managed to pay a rather lengthy visit to Farnley in 1812. The "Large Farnley" and "Woodcock Shooting" Sketch-Books (CXXVIII and CXXIX, Turner Bequest) seem to have been used on this occasion. The water-colour of *Woodcock Shooting* (painted for Sir H. Pilkington, and dated 1813), now in the Wallace Collection, represents a winding road among tall spruce firs, exactly like those which crown the rocky heights of the Otley Chevin. In the latter of these two sketch-books there are several pencil drawings of the fir trees on the slopes of the Chevin, with figures of beaters and sportsmen carrying guns. The former sketch-book contains drawings of Mr. Fawkes's tent on the Farnley moors, with dogs, guns, game, and ale barrels scattered in the foreground—notes from which the water-colour of this subject in the Farnley Collection was painted. Other pages of the same book contain beautiful drawings, some of them partly finished in colour, of Farnley and Wharfedale from Caley Park. Some loose leaves from this book were in the collection of the late Mr. J. E. Taylor, who presented one of them to Sir Frank Short.

In 1814 Turner was, I believe, too busy sketching the southern coast from Hastings to Margate, and his "Views in Sussex", to have much time for any lengthy visit to Farnley. But he was certainly there in 1815, as a passage in a letter to the Rev. H. Scott Trimmer proves. The letter is given in full in Monkhouse's "Turner" (p. 90). It is dated "Tuesday, Aug. 1, 1815." In it Turner says: "After next Tuesday—if you have a moment's time to spare, a line will reach me at Farnley Hall, near Otley, Yorkshire, and for some time, as Mr. Fawkes talks of keeping me in the north by a trip to the Lakes, &c., until November." The evidence of the sketch-books suggests that this trip to the Lakes did not take place.

On the 4th January, 1816, Mr. Walter Fawkes married his second wife, the widow of the Hon. and Rev. Pierce Butler. Fortunately for us this lady kept a diary, which has been carefully preserved at Farnley Hall, and which Mr. F. H. Fawkes has very kindly placed at my disposal. In this diary the names of all visitors were carefully noted, together with the dates of their arrival and departure. The diary was continued to the 31st December, 1838, but Turner's name does not occur in it after 1826. But for the ten years between 1816 and 1826 this diary forms an extremely valuable record of Turner's movements. I propose, therefore, with Mr. Fawkes's kind permission, to publish, for the first time, all the entries which have reference to the great artist.

The first entries of this kind are the following:—

"Wed.	17	July 1816.	Left Farnley with Walter, Maria, Amelia, Ayscough, Richard, and Mr. Turner. Met John Parker at Skipton, where we slept and saw Skipton Castle.
Thurs.	18	July	Arrived at Browsholme. Heavy rain.
Fri.	19	"	Rained all day. Sat in the house. Late in the evening walked a short way with John Parker and Mr. Turner.
Sat.	20	July	Walter drove me in curricle to the Trough of Bolland.
Sun.	21	"	Went to Waddington Church and after to see Mrs. Clarke.
Mon.	22	"	Went with the girls to the Trough to see them fish.
Tues.	23	"	Heavy rain. Drove with Walter. Obliged to take shelter in a farmhouse. Walter bought a print of the Prodigal Son.
Wed.	24	"	Left Browsholme. Got to Malham Village. Dreadful rain.
Thurs.	25	"	Went to see Gordale Waterfall. Returned home. Heavy rain. Turner went on a sketching tour."

From the frequent references to the rain it is evident that the weather was bad, and the lady does not seem to have enjoyed the excursion very much. But the weather did not prevent Turner from making the sketches he wanted. The sketch-book labelled by him "Yorkshire 2" (CXLV, Turner Bequest) contains the drawings made on this occasion. It is an ordinary-looking book, bound in boards, with brown leather back and corners. The leaves, which number nearly two hundred, are 6 in. × 3¾ in. size, but only a hundred and sixty of them have been drawn on. There are sketches of Skipton Castle at both ends of the book, showing that Turner was not at all particular about the order in which he made his sketches. The drawings on pages 160 to 185 represent views at Skipton, Browsholme, the Trough of Bolland (or Bowland, as it is generally written), and Gordale Scar. But they are all rather hurried in character, which corroborates Mrs. Fawkes's account of the unfavourable nature of the weather.

At the end of the book Turner has carefully made a list of the numbers and dates of the banknotes he carried with him to meet the expenses of his tour. He took two twenty-pound notes, four of ten pounds, five of five, and four smaller ones, making £110 in all. There is also, on the next page, a note of the expenses incurred on the journey from London to Leeds:—

"Porterage		2	8
Fare to Leeds	2	2	
Coachman		1	
Dinner at Eaton		5	6
Coachman—Scrooby		1	6
ditto		1	
Breakfast, Doncaster		2	3
Brandy and water, Grantham		1	6
Coachman and Guard		4	6
	3	2	11"

These items rather contradict Thornbury's statements about the extreme meanness and parsimony of the artist's habits of travel. I may also remark that the great painter's exuberant imagination has led him to overstate the total of his expenditure by the sum of one shilling.

Taking leave of his friends at Gordale, Turner set off by himself on a sketching tour to collect material for the illustrations to Dr. Whitaker's projected "History of Richmondshire." His sketch-book shows that he struck over the hills to Kilnsey Crag and then crossed the wild road from Wharfedale over the Stake Pass to Semmer Water. From Askrigg he made his way to Richmond. He was there on the 31st of July, as we find him on that date writing to Mr. Holworthy, saying that his "journey is extended, rather than shortened, by an excursion into Lancashire." The weather was still bad, as we learn from a characteristic postscript to this letter, which runs:—"Weather miserably wet. I shall be web-foot like a drake—excepting the curled feather—but I must proceed northward. Adieu." The sketch-book shows he did "proceed northward" as far as Barnard Castle, and then, turning into Westmorland, went south into Lancashire, after passing through Appleby to Kirkby Lonsdale and Heysham. Riding round Morecambe Bay, and probably crossing the sands at low tide, he seems to have got back to Farnley by about the middle of August.

The diary does not give the date of Turner's arrival at Farnley, but the shooting began on the 12th, when "all the gentlemen" went to the moors, and on the 13th an unfortunate gun accident wounded one of the party, Mr. Richard Hawksworth. On the 14th, the diary tells us that "Richard" was "pretty well;" on the 15th the entry runs, "Richard pretty well until evening. Sent for Hey" (the doctor), "who said he was dying." On the 16th "Poor Richard died at 5 o'clock in the morning." This sad event seems to have dispersed the house party, the entries on Saturday the 17th, and Monday 19th, recording the guests' departures. Only "Turner and John Parker remained and Miss Coates." On the 4th September Turner wrote from Farnley Hall to his correspondent, Mr. Holworthy, saying that "having finished nearly what I proposed doing this season in Yorkshire, I think I can do myself the pleasure of waiting upon Mr. Knight at Langold within a fortnight." This gentleman was evidently Mr. H. Gally Knight, whose sketch of the Temple of Jupiter in the Island of Ægina had formed the basis of Turner's large oil painting of this subject which was exhibited at the Royal Academy in 1816. Langold is two miles beyond Carlton, near Tickhill, Yorkshire. On the 11th September Turner writes to the same correspondent, saying that he intends to leave Farnley on "Sunday morning next" and that, if "Mr. Knight is not at Langold, I will be at Belvoir on the Tuesday following."

That Turner carried out at least the first part of his plan is proved by the entry in the diary, "Mr. Turner went away," under the date of Sunday, 15th September.

The water-colours Turner made from the sketches taken during this year are among the sunniest and happiest of his works. The lovely *Hornby Castle from Tatham Church* (now in the Victoria and Albert Museum), and the *Crook of the Lune* (in the Rev. W. Macgregor's collection) are perhaps the finest now existing of this series. But the happiness and pure enjoyment of life that breathe through these drawings must have been due to the artist's memories and associations, rather than to his actual experiences of the places represented, for the weather seems to have been consistently bad during the whole of this summer and autumn. In the letter to Mr. Holworthy referred to above, Turner wrote that his present trip had been "a most confounded fagg." Though he was on horseback, he added, "the passage out of Teesdale leaves everything far behind for difficulty—Bogged most compleatly, Horse and its Rider, and nine hours making 11 miles." And in another part of the same letter, he wrote, "As to weather, there is nothing inviting, it must be confessed. Rain, rain, rain, day after day. Italy deluged, Switzerland a wash-pot, Neufchatel, Berne and Morat Lakes all in *one*—all chance of getting over the Simplon or any of the passes *now* vanished like the morning mist." So the writer had evidently nursed some project of going to Italy in the latter part of this year, a project which he was not able to carry out till two years later.

The year 1817 saw the addition of a very important series of fifty drawings to Mr. Walter Fawkes's already large collection. These were the famous Rhine drawings. The date of their execution is given incorrectly in Thornbury, but the newly-discovered evidence of the sketch-books and an entry in Mrs. Fawkes's diary enable us to correct Thornbury's inaccuracies. Thornbury says these drawings "were done at the prodigious rate of three a day," and in support of this statement he adds that Turner was away only for a fortnight, and that "after landing at Hull he came straight to Farnley, where, even before taking off his great-coat, he produced the drawings, in a slovenly roll from his breast pocket; and Mr. Fawkes bought the lot for some £500, doubtless to Turner's delight, for he could not bear that any series of his should be broken." But a kind of rough diary of Turner's movements in the "Itinerary Rhine Tour Sketch-Book" (CLIX, Turner Bequest) says that the artist "left London" on Sunday, 10th August, was "off Margate" on Monday, 11th, and reached Brussels Thursday evening, on the 14th. He spent Saturday, visiting the Field of Waterloo, and, taking the diligence on Sunday, passed through Liège and Aix-la-Chapelle, reaching Cologne on the 18th. On Tuesday he walked to Bonn, and on the following day to Remagen. He was at Coblenz on Thursday and Friday, the 21st and 22nd, at St. Goar on the next two days, and at Mayence on the 25th and 26th. He returned to St. Goar on the 27th, and, passing through Coblenz on the 28th, he reached Cologne on the 29th, and left it the next day, returning through Aix and Liège. He was at Antwerp on the 2nd and 3rd of September, and at Rotterdam on the 4th and 5th, from whence he made his way to The Hague and Amsterdam. The notes against the dates to the 15th September are too elliptical and undecipherable to convey any information, but even if the artist did take the boat from Holland to Hull (the most probable route of his return) immediately on or after this date, it is clear that he did not go straight from there to Farnley. He had some work to do in Durham before he could go there—sketches to make of Gibside and Hylton Castle, the seats of the Earl of Strathmore, and of Raby Castle, the seat of the Earl of Darlington, to illustrate Surtees' "History of the County of Durham." He had also a commission to paint a large oil picture of the latter castle for its owner, a picture which duly appeared on the walls of the Royal Academy in the following year. A passage in a letter to Mr. Holworthy, written on the 21st November, 1817, says that "Lord Strathmore call'd at Raby and took me away to the North," thus keeping him in Durham longer than he had expected. In this way Turner did not reach Farnley till the middle of November. Mrs. Fawkes's diary tells us that she and her husband "went to Thorp Ash" on Thursday, 13th November, and on the 15th the entry runs, "Heavy rain. Returned home. Found Mr. Turner and Greaves here." It is evident that Turner stayed there for about a week, as the letter of the 21st November is dated from Farnley Hall, but it is probable that he did not remain much longer, as he was clearly anxious to get back home and to work, for he says in this letter, "The season is far spent, the night of winter near at hand, and Barry's words are always ringing in my ears—'Get home and light your lamp.'"

The object of Thornbury's statements about Turner being away only for a fortnight, and going straight to Farnley after landing at Hull, is evidently to corroborate his assertion that the fifty drawings were done "at the prodigious rate of three a day." No one who has studied these beautiful drawings at all carefully could believe such a statement. But the evidence of Turner's own memoranda proves that he only spent twelve days visiting the places on the Rhine which he has represented. He occupied from the 18th of August to the 30th sketching between Cologne and Mayence. So if we look at the matter from Thornbury's point of view we are entitled to say that the fifty water-colours were done, not at the prodigious rate of three a day, but at the prodigious rate of more than four a day. But such a conclusion clearly overlooks the important difference between a sketch from nature and a finished drawing. In the twelve days Turner spent on the Rhine he certainly made the sketches for the fifty drawings Mr. Fawkes bought; and, in addition, he also made the sketches—numbering something between a hundred and fifty and two hundred—which we find in the three sketch-books, "Itinerary Rhine Tour," "Waterloo and Rhine," and "The Rhine" (CLIX, CLX, CLXI, Turner Bequest), preserved in the National Gallery. But it is evident the Farnley water-colours were not painted from nature. They were elaborated from pencil sketches somewhere between the end of August and the 13th November, possibly at inns—for Turner could work anywhere and under any conditions—or possibly when staying with Lord Darlington at Raby Castle, or with Lord Strathmore at Hylton Castle or Gibside. Such drawings as *Johannesberg*, *Sonneck and Baccharach*, *Mayence and Cassel*, and the rest, are not hurried sketches from nature, but carefully pondered and perfectly elaborated works of art. In some few cases parts of the sky or distance may have been painted from nature, but they all owe much of their charm and beauty to the consummately skilful labour which the artist lavished upon them in the intervals of travel, during the two months which elapsed between his departure from Cologne and his arrival at Farnley Hall near the beginning of November.

When Turner wrote to Mr. Holworthy from Farnley Hall, "The season is far spent, the night of winter near at hand, and Barry's words are always ringing in my ears—'Get home and light your lamp,'" his mind was evidently full of ideas of pictures he was anxious to carry out. The subject-matter of three important oil paintings—the large view of *Raby Castle* for the Earl of Darlington, the serenely beautiful evening effect of *The Dort Packet-Boat from*

Rotterdam becalmed, which he painted for Mr. Fawkes (and which is shown hanging over the fireplace, in the position it still occupies to-day, in the water-colour of *The Drawing-room at Farnley*, which was reproduced and published in the March number of THE STUDIO), and the imaginative composition of *The Field of Waterloo*, showing the ground

"Covered thick with other clay
Which her own clay shall cover, heaped and pent
Rider and horse, friend, foe, in one red burial blent."

—was seething in his mind and crying out for definite embodiment. These pictures were ready for exhibition at the Royal Academy in May 1818. In June Mr. Fawkes and his wife were in London. Two of Mr. Fawkes's sons by his first marriage were at Eton, so we find the following entry in Mrs. Fawkes's diary on the 4th of June: "Went to Eton to see the boat-race. Dined and slept at Salt Hill. Little Turner came with us." That "little" Turner's thoughts were not taken up entirely with the boat-race and the social pleasures of the visit is proved by the lovely sepia drawing of *Windsor Castle from Salt Hill*, which was admirably engraved by Charles Turner for the "Liber Studiorum," though it was never published. Soon after this visit to Eton Turner went to Scotland to make sketches to illustrate "The Provincial Antiquities of Scotland," for which Sir Walter Scott (then plain Mr. Scott) had agreed to furnish the letterpress. Scott would have preferred the employment of his friend the Rev. John Thomson, of Duddingston, as the illustrator of this work, but Lockhart and the publishers stood out for Turner. Scott finally gave way and wrote that he "supposed he must acquiesce" in the selection of Turner, "because he was all the fashion." Turner's subjects were chosen for him and the work proved remarkably successful. Turner's exquisite water-colours were presented by the publishers to Sir Walter Scott, who had them all framed together (in a very unsuitable way, it must be confessed) and kept them hung in his study at Abbotsford until his death.

There is no mention in the diary of any visit of Turner to Farnley Hall in 1818, but it is probable that he called there on his way back from Scotland. The water-colour of *A First Rater taking in Stores*, which is said to have been painted at Farnley Hall, is dated 1818. The water-colour drawing of *The Drawing-room at Farnley*, to which I have already referred, must also have been painted that year, as the picture of *Dort* could not have been in its place before then, and the drawing was included in the exhibition of Turner's works which Mr. Fawkes held in April 1819.

To appreciate fully the importance of this exhibition it will be necessary for us to glance for a moment at the conditions of artistic patronage in this country during the earlier years of the nineteenth century. As we had no

National Gallery then, opportunities for becoming familiar with the works of the great European painters of the past were extremely limited. With a view to educating the taste of the public, some of the artists made the suggestion that the nobility and gentry, who owned collections of works by the old masters, should admit the public to their galleries or houses on a certain day in each week during the fashionable season. The Marquess of Stafford and Earl Grosvenor acted upon this suggestion. But after a time complaints were made that the taste for the old masters was prejudicial to the claims for recognition of the living native artists of the day. To redress the balance Lord de Tabley, who had formed a fine collection of exclusively British paintings, decided to throw open his gallery to the public. Many of his friends tried to dissuade him from doing this, as they thought that the British School could not emerge with credit from the inevitable comparisons which would be made with the more famous Schools of the Continent. But he invited and allowed the public to visit his gallery on one day in the week during the season of 1818. His experiment was so successful that it was repeated the following year. William Carey, a dealer who had assisted Lord de Tabley in forming his collection, tells us that "the splendour of the British School produced a favourable conviction on the minds of foreign visitors. The effect was indescribable. It increased on each year of the exhibition, and the periodical press, in bearing testimony to the general enthusiasm which seized all the upper classes, rapidly spread the fame of the British School through the Empire" ("Some Memoirs of the Patronage and Progress of the Fine Arts," &c., published in 1826). The success of Lord de Tabley's bold experiment seems to have suggested to Mr. Walter Fawkes the idea of admitting the public to see the large collection of English water-colours he had formed. The writer referred to above tells us that he "had the pleasure of hearing Mr. Fawkes mention his intended exhibition to a small circle of amateurs, with a doubt whether the public would approve of paintings in water-colours without any pictures in oil. Some gentlemen replied hesitatingly; but the approbation of His Royal Highness the Duke of Gloucester, who was present, determined the question. Lord de Tabley gave the plan his instant and warm concurrence. Mr. Thomas Lister Parker, of Browsholme Hall, was equally prompt in his assent. The drawings were first displayed in an evening when the apartments were judicially illuminated. Mr. Fawkes issued cards of invitation for the private view only, and, notwithstanding that he was particularly select, the spacious suite of rooms was too small to receive the company. The effect was very striking. It was generally remarked that Grosvenor Place never before beheld such a blaze of beauty of fashion, or such a splendid assemblage of distinguished public characters, as on that evening, and on the subsequent days of exhibition."

The first and second rooms of the suite were filled with drawings by De Wint, J. C. Ibbetson, T. Heaphy, Glover, Havell, Robson, Hills, Prout, Atkinson, and Warwick Smith. The principal apartment, the largest in size and the last to be entered, was hung entirely with drawings by Turner. I will not venture to quote Carey's rhapsodical description of these drawings. It is every whit as rapturous and enthusiastic as any of the purple patches penned by "A Graduate of Oxford" some fourteen or fifteen years later, but it has nothing of Ruskin's eloquence or felicity of literary expression. Still the following remarks, from Carey's useful book, are, I think, worth quoting: "Turner the enchanter, whose magic pencil had created the chief wonders of this temple, was frequently there. Nature, in endowing his mind, appears to have been indifferent to his person; but his brow is a page on which the traits of his high calling are stamped in capital letters, and his dark eyes sparkle with the fires of inspiration. He generally came alone; and while he leaned on the centre table in the great room, or slowly worked his rough way through the mass, he attracted every eye in the brilliant crowd, and seemed to me like a victorious Roman General, the principal figure in his own triumph. Perhaps no British artist ever retired from an exhibition of his works, with so much reason for unmixed satisfaction, or more genuine proofs of well-deserved admiration from the public." Carey adds, "It is more than seven years since I saw this extraordinary exhibition; and even now the remembrance affects me...." And after a page or two of rather turgid bombast he winds up with the naïve remark, "I own I am an enthusiastic worshipper of Turner's genius."

The references to Turner in Mrs. Fawkes's diary for this time are extremely limited. We learn from it that the family came to the house in Grosvenor Place in March. On Sunday, 7th March, the entry runs: "Went with girls to Belgrave Chapel. Mr. Parker, Alston, Turner, and Mr. Miller dined with us." The entry on Tuesday, 13th April, is: "Very wet day, Gallery opened in Grosvenor Place. 1st day." During the next few weeks a number of dinner parties are recorded, but no names of the guests are mentioned. We may take it for granted that Turner was frequently present on these occasions.

After the exhibition Mr. Fawkes had a catalogue published of the drawings included in the show. The catalogue was dedicated "To J. M. W. Turner, Esq., R.A., P.P.," in the following graceful letter:—

"My dear Sir,

"The unbought and spontaneous expression of the public opinion respecting my collection of water-colour drawings decidedly points out to whom this little catalogue should be inscribed. To you, therefore, I dedicate it: first, as an act of duty, and secondly, as an Offering of Friendship: for be assured I never can look at it without intensely feeling the delight I have experienced during the greater part of my life from the exercise of your talent, and the pleasure of your society.

"That you may year after year reap an accession of fame and fortune is the anxious wish of

"Your sincere friend,
W. FAWKES."

"London, June, 1819.

The family copy of this catalogue was illustrated with a frontispiece and two water-colours by Turner, one a view of *London from the Windows of 45, Grosvenor Place*, the other a view of the *Drawing-room of 45, Grosvenor Place*.

To understand properly the importance of this exhibition to Turner's reputation as a water-colour painter, we must bear in mind that since his election as a member of the Royal Academy he had been known to the public primarily as an oil painter; and he had held aloof from the newly-established Water-Colour Society, and had, therefore, no regular opportunities for submitting his water-colour drawings to the public. Mr. Fawkes's friendly exhibition, held under the most fortunate social conditions, firmly established Turner's position as the foremost water-colour painter of his time, and enabled him to produce, during the next twenty years, those marvellous series of drawings which are so eagerly sought after by collectors of the present day, and so warmly appreciated and enjoyed by all who care for the higher achievements of the Fine Arts.

In the summer of 1819 Turner paid his first visit to Italy. He went from Calais to Paris, followed the usual coach route to Turin, and, having explored the north Italian lakes, he reached Venice by way of Milan and Brescia. He must have spent some time in Venice to judge from the large number of sketches he made there. Making his way along the coast of the Adriatic he turned inland at Ancona, and following the high post road through Recanati and Macerata, entered the Via Flaminia at Foligno, and saw Rome for the first time, probably some time in September or October. From Rome he explored Frascati and Tivoli, and made a tour to Naples, Pompeii and Herculaneum. He left Rome in December, visited Florence, and re-crossed the Alps on the 24th January 1820. He returned through Piedmont and France, and we find him dining at Grosvenor Place with the Fawkses on Saturday, 12th February. During the next few months he must have been frequently in the society of his friends, as his name constantly recurs in the entries of Mrs. Fawkes's diary. The following extracts will speak for themselves:—

"Monday,	14th	Feb., 1820.	Went a large party to see the Panorama of Lausanne. Turner and Mr. Lomax dined with us.
Sunday,	27th	Feb.	B. King, E. Parker, Turner, Mr. Lomax and W. Beaumont dined with us.
Sunday,	9th	April.	Drove out with Walter to Whitly and Turner's Garden. E. Parker dined with us.
Sunday,	30th	April.	Mr. Swinburne, Parker, Turner dined with us.
Sunday,	7th	May.	Walter out in Phaeton. Mr. Swinburne, Parker, Turner and Alston and Mills dined with us.
Sunday,	21st	May.	Lord Belmore came to pay a visit. Maria and I went to Warwick St. Chapel. Turner and Swinburne dined with us.
Monday,	5th	June.	Walter, two of the girls, and I went to Salt Hill. Saw the Boat Race. Young Knight fell from his horse. Broke his arm. Fine day. Wet afternoon. Mr. Swinburne and Turner.
Tuesday,	4th	July.	To Greenwich. Traceys, Mr. and Mrs. Alston, Turner, Sir Francis D. Kinnaird. All the party drank tea in Grosvenor Place. Fine day, not hot."

Turner's visit to Italy did not have a very beneficial effect upon his art. He came back with a mass of material and then seems to have been puzzled to know what to do with it all. The *Bay of Baiæ*, the first important oil painting which he produced after this visit, is overloaded with detail, and the design possesses no organic unity. The best artistic results of the journey were a few water-colours painted for Mr. Fawkes. The *Rialto, Venice*, a brilliant drawing, though overcrowded with facts, is interesting as Turner's first Venetian picture done from his own sketches—the drawing of the same subject engraved in Hakewill's "Italy" having been made from camera-obscura tracings furnished by Hakewill. The *Interior of St. Peter's, Rome*, is a wonderful drawing, remarkable for the sense of height and space obtained by taking deliberate liberties with the laws of perspective. The view of *The Colosseum, Rome*, is exquisite in colour and effect. The best inspired of all the drawings produced this year (1820) is, however, *The Passage of Mont Cenis*, in which the contrast between the frightened passengers in the diligence, with its wildly plunging horses, and the gleaming peaks of the frozen mountains, is emphasized with extraordinary skill and eloquence.

These drawings practically completed the Farnley Hall collection. Turner's friendship with Mr. Fawkes continued unabated till the latter's death in 1825, but the only drawings added to the collection after 1820 are interesting rather on private and personal grounds than for their artistic importance. They are mere records of relics of the Civil War preserved at Farnley, or vignette illustrations, the poetical or historical compilations with which members of the Fawkes family amused their leisure.

I do not think I can better conclude this account of Turner's personal relations with Mr. Walter Fawkes than by placing on record the remaining entries in Mrs. Fawkes's diary in which the artist is either directly or indirectly referred to.

In 1821 the family came to Mr. Fawkes's London house on Wednesday, 21st March, "at 4 o'clock." The next day, Thursday, "Turner and Parker dined with us." On Thursday, 21st June, the entry runs: "Went to Eton with Walter, the girls, Mr. Swinburne and Turner." The family left London on 23rd July, and Turner does not seem to have seen them till he went up to Farnley to spend Christmas with them. "Mr. Turner came" is entered against Sunday, 23rd December, but the date of his departure is not given.

In 1822 the family arrived at Grosvenor Place on 10th April. On Sunday, the 14th, "Mr. Alston, Turner and G. Wentworth dined with us." The 20th of June was a great day for the family. On that day Miss Anne Fawkes, the youngest of Mr. Fawkes's daughters by his first marriage, was married to Mr. Godfrey Wentworth, of Woolley Park, co. York. There were twenty-three guests present at the dinner given in honour of this event, among them several Lords and Ladies and "Mr. Turner." The entry in the diary on this day is brief but eloquent. It runs: "Anne and Godfrey married. A very long day. Had a large party to dinner. All tipsey."

Turner's name does not appear in the diary during the whole of 1823, nor in 1824 till the end of the year, when he went to Farnley for nearly a month. The following entries speak for themselves:—

"Friday,	19	Nov.	1824.	Turner came.
Tuesday,	14	Dec.	"	Mr. Turner went away.
Monday,	3	Jan.	1825.	Left Farnley for Baker Street.
Thursday,	6	"	"	Arrived in London.

Saturday,	8	”	”	Mr. Parker and Turner came to dinner.
Sunday,	9	”	”	Foggy, nasty day. Mr. Turner dined with us.
Sunday,	16	”	”	Mr. Turner dined with us.
Sunday,	30	”	”	Walked to Hanover Square to see the Wentworths. Mr. Turner dined with us.
Monday,	31	”	”	Mr. Sapio came to teach Eliza. Hawksworth went to Windsor. Turner and Mr. Woodhouse dined with us. H.'s birthday.
Sunday,	6	Feb.	”	Turner dined with us.
Sunday,	20	”	”	Mr. Lister, Turner and Dr. Bree dined.
Wednesday,	2	March	”	Walter's birthday. Charles and Fanny Brandling, Mr. Creevy, Turner, Mr. Alston and Rowland dined with us.
Sunday,	13	March,	1825.	Mr. Parker and Mr. Turner dined with us and John Ibbetson and Mr. Wharton.
Sunday,	3	April	”	Turner, Anne and Godfrey dined with us. * * * Went to Baker Street Chapel with Fanny and Eliza.
Wednesday,	6	”	”	Hawksworth and Eliza married at St. George's by the A. bishop of York. We had a large dinner party and the Infant Lyra in the evening.
Sunday,	17	”	”	Fanny B. and Hawkey called. Drove with Fanny Brandling to Mr. Clarke's house. His first visit. T. Parker and Turner dined with us.
Friday,	22	”	”	Tom Parker and Mr. Turner dined with us. A ball at Mrs. Stanhope's. Did not go.

Sunday,	1	May,	1825.	Ill. Mr. Lister, C. Brandling, Edward Parker and Mr. Turner dined with us.
Sunday,	15	,,	,,	Mr. Wodehouse and Turner dined with us. Ayscough came from Oxford.
Friday,	3	June	,,	Walter was this evening condemned to his bed. He kissed me and cried bitterly. Came back several times to kiss and said he knew he never more should get out of it. I passed a wretched night.
Sunday,	14	Aug.	,,	Mr. Alston and Turner dined.
Saturday,	27	,,	,,	Turner dined in Baker Street. Said he was going next morning to the Hague."

This entry enables us to date with certainty the "Holland Sketch-Book" (CCXIV) in the National Gallery. Mr. Walter Fawkes died on the 25th of October of this year, probably before Turner got back to London from his tour in Holland.

Mrs. Fawkes spent a few days in London in May the following year, and Turner dined with her on two occasions, on Tuesday the 2nd and Sunday the 7th of May. The diary was continued till 31st December, 1838, but I can find no further mention in it of Turner's name.

Thornbury says, "Turner was so sensitive that he could never make up his mind to visit Farnley after his old friend's death." And we have Ruskin's testimony that Turner could never speak of the Wharfe, about whose shores the shadows of old thoughts and long-lost delights hung like morning mist, but his voice faltered.

TURNER'S RELATIONS WITH MR. H. FAWKES

ON the death of Mr. Walter Fawkes Farnley Hall passed to his son, Mr. Francis Hawksworth Fawkes. He was a boy when Turner first became friendly with the family. He had romped, walked, shot with Turner, and had sat at his elbow while he was making many of the wonderful drawings in the Farnley Collection. No doubt young Hawksworth was one of the party in the carriage which Turner insisted upon driving tandem from the shooting tent on the Farnley moors, and which he managed to capsize "amid shouts of good-humoured laughter"—an exploit which earned the artist the nickname of "Over-Turner." It was to young "Hawkey" that Turner called one day in 1810, when he stood on the terrace at Farnley watching the storm rolling and shafting out its lightning over the Wharfedale hills—the storm effect he was to paint in his picture of *Hannibal Crossing the Alps*. The same boy sat watching him for three hours as he sat one morning between breakfast and lunch-time making the beautiful drawing of *A First-Rater taking in Stores*, the artist all the time "working like a madman" and "tearing up the sea with the eagle-claw of a thumbnail." It was young Hawksworth who induced his father to buy the large oil painting of *Dort* from the exhibition of 1818.

After Turner's death, Mr. Hawksworth Fawkes furnished Thornbury with the following account of his connection with the great artist. "When Turner was so much here (at Farnley) in my father's lifetime, I was but a boy, and not of an age to appreciate or interest myself in the workings of his mind or pencil. My recollection of him in those days refers to the fun, frolic, and shooting we enjoyed together, and which, whatever may be said by others of his temper and disposition, have proved to me that he was, in his hours of distraction from his professional labours, as kindly-minded a man and as capable of enjoyment and fun of all kinds as any that I ever knew.

"Though often invited, Turner never came here after my father's death; and, as I have seldom gone to London, our meetings since I had learnt his value had been few and far between: but up to the last time that I saw him, about a year before his death, he was always the same to me that I had known him in my boyhood, always addressed me by my boy name, and seemed ever anxious to express in his kindness to me his attachment to my father, and still glowing recollections of his 'auld lang syne' here."

Thornbury says that when Mr. Hawksworth Fawkes visited London "he would go and sit in the Queen Anne Street gallery for hours, but he was never shown into the painting-room. On one occasion he invited Turner to dinner at a London hotel, when he took, as was his wont latterly, a great deal too much wine. For once he became vain, and, staggering about, exclaimed, 'Hawkey, I am the real lion—I am the great lion of the day, Hawkey.'"

After Mr. Walter Fawkes's death one of those wonders of the North, a goose-pie and presents of game were sent to Turner from Farnley regularly at Christmas time. The twenty-fifth pie was already packed when the news reached Farnley of the painter's death. The three last letters Turner wrote to Mr. Fawkes acknowledging these annual presents have been preserved and published. In the one written on the 24th December, 1849, Turner finishes by saying: "I am sorry to say my health is much on the wane. I cannot bear the same fatigue, or have the same bearing against it, I formerly had—but time and tide stop not—but I must stop writing for to-day, and so I again beg to thank you for the Christmas present." In the letter dated 17th December, 1850, the aged artist wrote: "Old Time has made sad work with me since I saw you in town. I always dread it with horror now. I feel it acutely now, whatever (it is)—gout or nervousness—it has fallen into my pedestals, and bid adieu to the marrow-bone stage." These words, and indeed all the letter, are written in Turner's curiously involved and confused style, but it was evident that the great painter's career was nearly run. He died on the 9th December of the following year, and was buried eleven days later in the crypt of St. Paul's beside Sir Joshua Reynolds, with all the magnificence due to his genius.

THE FARNLEY HALL COLLECTION

IT will be seen from the foregoing account of the personal relations between Mr. Walter Fawkes and Turner that the Farnley Hall Collection is mainly concerned with Turner's work between the years 1804 and 1821. These works, therefore, belong to what Mr. Ruskin has described as Turner's first period, when "he laboured as a student, imitating successively the works of the various masters who excelled in the qualities he desired to attain himself." This classification of Mr. Ruskin's is evidently made in the interests of Turner's later work, the period Mr. Ruskin admired most. But the *parti-pris* and insufficiency of a classification which dismisses the period during which the paintings and drawings of the Farnley Hall Collection were produced as one of mere imitation of the old masters are sufficiently exposed by a glance at the illustrations with which the present publication is enriched. To speak of the creator of the *The Passage of Mont Cenis, Scarborough, Otley from the Chevin,* and *The Valley of the Wharfe from Caley Park* as a mere imitator seems to me quite absurd. My own view is that Turner's period of imitation and apprenticeship had come to an end by the time he was thirty years of age (1805). By that time he was a complete master of every form of pictorial expression. The period between his thirtieth and forty-fifth years was the period of his freshest and happiest inspiration, as well as that of his soundest and most perfect workmanship. His oil paintings produced during these years are as solidly and carefully worked as those of the old Flemish and Dutch masters. They are built to defy the centuries. A picture like the so-called *Pilot Boat (Shoeburyness Fisherman hailing a Whitstable Hoy)*—painted more than a hundred years ago—is a model of perfect craftsmanship. It has no cracks, and Time has only mellowed the exquisite pearly harmonies of its colour and the indescribable charm of its wonderful surface. The *Trout Stream,* the *Spithead,* and *Frosty Morning,* have the same gift of immortality. It is only Turner's later paintings which have cracked and faded and tarnished, and lost the "unthrifty loveliness" with which they were dowered when they were first exhibited.

I may, I hope, be pardoned for preferring the classification of Turner's "periods" adopted in my study of "Turner's Sketches and Drawings" to Mr. Ruskin's sweeping generalization. Turner's Farnley work impinges on three of these periods—it begins with that of 1802 to 1809, when Turner was producing his own glorious sea-pieces; it covers the next period, from 1809 to 1813, when Turner was developing that deep and solemn conception of the poetry of rural life, which found expression in the *Frosty Morning*, *Abingdon* and *Windsor*; and it runs half-way into the period of Turner's greatest academical and popular success—that of 1813 to 1830. Of these three phases of Turner's dazzling and complex genius I regard the middle one as the most important. The works produced in those years founded a genuinely national school of homely realism, and show Turner as the leader and inspirer of the Norwich School, and the master of David Cox, De Wint and all that is best in English water-colour painting. The spirit which animated this period is the spirit which informs nearly all the oil paintings and water-colours in the Farnley Hall Collection.

At the death of Mr. Walter Fawkes, Turner's works at Farnley Hall consisted of seven oil paintings and about two hundred water-colours. Since then the collection has been reduced to about two-thirds of its original size. Various drawings have been given as presents to different members of the family, and accidents of various kinds have happened to a few of the drawings. One of Mr. Walter Fawkes's sons was given a couple of drawings to decorate his room at Eton. One of the drawings got dirtied and the boy put it in a basin of water to clean it, with disastrous results—a very expensive way of learning the difference between an oil painting and a water-colour. But the biggest gap in the collection was made by one of the present owner's predecessors, the Rev. Ayscough Fawkes, who sent forty-nine water-colours and three oil paintings to Christie's in June, 1890.

No complete list of the original collection has yet been published. The following list is as nearly exhaustive as I have been able to make it. I have broken this list up into eight groups for convenience of reference, viz., (1) The oil paintings, (2) The early Swiss drawings, (3) The Rhine drawings, (4) Yorkshire, marine and other subjects,(5) The Wharfedale Series, (6) Birds, (7) Vignettes, (8) Italian and later Swiss drawings. Where the works have passed from the possession of Mr. F. H. Fawkes, the present owner of the collection, I have indicated in brackets the collection into which they have passed, or the latest appearance in the sale-room or exhibition of which I have a record. Where there is no entry in brackets after the title the work is still at Farnley Hall.

THE OIL PAINTINGS.

1. London from Greenwich Park. 36" × 48". (National Gallery, No. 483.)

2. Shoeburyness Fisherman hailing a Whitstable Hoy—sometimes called Pilot with Red Cap hailing a Smack in Stormy Weather. 36" × 48".

3. The *Victory* returning from Trafalgar, beating up Channel in three positions: fresh breeze. 27" × 40". (Christie's, 1890; Sir Donald Currie.)

4. Scene in the Apennines, with peasants driving sheep. 13½" × 19¼"—panel. (Christie's, 1890; E. L. Raphael, Esq. Exhibited R. A. 1892; Guildhall, 1899.)

5. The Sun rising in a Mist. 27" × 40". (Christie's, 1890; Mrs. Johnstone Foster.)

6. The Lake of Geneva, from above Vevey, and looking towards the Valley of the Rhone. 41½" × 65¼". (Christie's, 1890; Sir Donald Currie.)

7. Dort, or Dordrecht—the Dort Packet-boat from Rotterdam becalmed. Signed and dated "J. M. W. Turner, R.A., 1818, Dort." Exhibited R.A. 1818. 62" × 91½".

8. Rembrandt's Daughter. Exhibited R.A. 1827. 46½" × 44½".

A free rendering of the *London from Greenwich Park* was engraved in the "Liber Studiorum" and published 1st January, 1811. The plate is inscribed, "Picture in the possession of Walter Fawkes, Esq., of Farnley." Turner must, however, have bought back or exchanged the picture, as it was in his gallery at the time of his death, and thus passed into the National Gallery. Soon after its first exhibition at Marlborough House, in 1856, Mr. Ruskin published a curious "note" upon it, bewailing in eloquent terms the fact that Turner should waste his genius upon such an unworthy subject as London and a view of the Thames. "What a sorrowful matter it is," he explained, that there was no one who "had sense and feeling enough" to tell Turner to paint the Rhone instead of the Thames, the Simplon instead of Richmond Hill, and Rouen Cathedral instead of Greenwich Hospital. Turner found his way at last to these subjects, Mr. Ruskin added, "but not till many and many a year had been wasted on Greenwich and Bligh Sands." We need not on the present occasion trouble to examine too curiously the reasons which induced Mr. Ruskin to take such an entirely perverse view of the kind of subjects an English landscape painter ought to choose. It is sufficient to point out that an artist can only paint with his full power those scenes which he knows and loves intimately. Turner was born in London, and the Thames with its shipping about London Bridge stirred Turner's imagination with memories of his boyhood, his early dreams and aspirations, in a way that the Rhone, or the Rhine, or the Danube could never stir it. No doubt these rivers are broader and deeper than the Thames, fairer to the eye of the tourist, and richer in historical associations; but these advantages are no compensation for that affectionate intimacy which guides and inspires the artist when he is dealing with scenes familiar to him since his boyhood. I will not hesitate to assert that Turner's paintings and drawings of his native land and its rivers and ports stir my imagination and emotions far more powerfully and harmoniously than those of foreign parts. In spite of the tranquil splendour of the Farnley *Dort*, the magnificence of Mr. Naylor's *Cologne* and Mr. Ralph Brocklebank's *Ehrenbreitstein*, and the intricate play of cunning line and gorgeous colour in the water-colour of *Heidelberg* (in the Donald Currie Collection), I would not exchange any of these works for the sober harmonies and beautiful feeling of *London from Greenwich Park*, or the more moving drama of the fisherman's daily life on the Thames enshrined in the *Shoeburyness Fisherman hailing a Whitstable Hoy*.

The picture of the *Victory* returning from Trafalgar was painted about the same time as the *Shoeburyness Fisherman*. It is hallowed by association with Nelson's glorious end, but it is lacking in that unity and energy of pictorial motive which make the *Shoeburyness Fisherman* such a masterpiece of sea-painting.

Rembrandt's Daughter is the only picture in the Farnley Collection which was bought by Mr. Walter Fawkes's son, Mr. Hawksworth Fawkes. It was not well chosen. It shows Turner as an imitator and humble admirer of other artists, rather than as the great creative genius he was. It is not a typical work of the artist, but it throws an interesting side-light on the moods of hesitation and tentative experiment in which he occasionally indulged. Rembrandt and his wife are supposed to be surprising their daughter—an entirely mythical personage—while she is reading a love-letter. There are some fine passages of colour in the girl's dress. The picture was exhibited at the Royal Academy in 1827.

EARLY SWISS DRAWINGS.

9. Glacier and Source of the Arveiron, going up to the Mer de Glace. Exhibited R.A. 1803. 27" × 40".

10. The Great Fall of the Reichenbach; in the valley of Hasle, Switzerland. Signed and dated "J. M. W. Turner, R.A., 1804." Exhibited R.A. 1815. 40" × 27". (Plate IX.)

11. The Passage of Mount St. Gothard; taken from the centre of the Teufels Broch (Devil's Bridge), Switzerland. Signed and dated "J. M. W. Turner, R.A., 1804." Exhibited R.A. 1815. 40½" × 27".

12. Blair's Hut on the Montanvert, and Mer de Glace, Chamounix. 11" × 15".

13. The Valley of Chamounix. Signed and dated "J. M. W. Turner, R.A., p.p., 1809(?)." 11¼ × 15⅝". (Plate III.)

14. Lake of Thun. 11" × 15½".

15. The Staubbach, Valley of Lauterbrunnen. Signed and dated "J. M. W. Turner, 1809." 11" × 15".

16. The Lake of Brienz: Moonlight. Signed "J. M. W. Turner, R.A." 11" × 15½". (Plate XII.)

17. Bonneville, Savoy. 11" × 15⅜". (Plate I.)

18. Vevey, Lake of Geneva. 11" × 15½". (Christie's, 1890; Sir Donald Currie.)

19. Sallenches. 11" × 15½". (Christie's, 1890; Humphrey Roberts's sale, May, 1908.)

20. Chamounix; Mer de Glace. 11" × 13½". (Christie's, 1890; Humphrey Roberts's sale, May, 1908.)

21. Lausanne and Lake of Geneva. 11¼" × 15½". Signed and dated "J. M. W. Turner, R.A., 1807." (Christie's, 1890; A. J. Forbes-Leith, Esq.)

22. Source of the Arveiron. 11" × 15½". (Christie's, 1890; Turner House, Penarth, Pyke-Thompson Bequest.)

23. Lake of Lucerne, from Flüelen. 26½" × 39½". (Christie's, 1890; Sir Donald Currie.)

24. MontBlanc, from the Vald'Aosta. 26" × 39½". (Christie's, 1810; Sir Donald Currie.)

All these drawings were based on sketches made during Turner's first tour in Savoy and Switzerland, in 1802. The earliest are dated 1803 and 1804, others were executed four or five years later, and a few may not have been completed till about 1815. They evidently owe a great deal to the inspiration of Richard Wilson and Nicholas Poussin, though we find in them that same large and masculine grip of natural form and structure which we see in pictures like the *Bridgewater Sea-Piece* and *Calais Pier*. In some of the drawings, indeed—the *Great Fall of the Reichenbach* and *The Passage of Mount St. Gothard*, for instance—the calm, unhurried elaboration of rock forms gives them a certain cold and prosaic air. Such drawings lack the gloomy majesty and lyrical intensity of feeling of paintings like *The Trossachs*, *Conway Castle* and *Kilgarran Castle*. For work of this kind a certain vagueness and generalisation of execution are necessary, and Turner was, after 1804, already beginning to feel his way towards a greater clarity and lucidity of expression than Wilson had attempted. The Farnley drawings represent, therefore, what I may call the aftermath of Turner's early romantic mood. They are conceived under the influence of that taste for the gloomy, mysterious and picturesque fostered by Milton, Young's "Night Thoughts," and Walpole's "Castle of Otranto"; but the fulness of representation and cheerful and varied colour of their execution are not altogether in harmony with their original intention. In these respects the original sketches of *The Pass of St. Gothard* in the National Gallery (LXXXV, 33, 34, and 35) are more satisfactory to the imagination than the larger and more elaborate drawing in the Farnley Collection. The absence of romantic passion is, however, atoned for by the stateliness and grandeur of the design.

The two drawings of this group which make the strongest appeal to my feelings are the moonlit view of The *Lake of Brienz* and the gloomy and majestic *Glacier and Source of the Arveiron* which was exhibited at the Royal Academy in 1803. Both these drawings are darker and more Wilsonesque in colour and effect than the others. The starkness and bigness of drawing in the group of pine trees in the foreground of the *Glacier and Source of the Arveiron* strike the imagination with Miltonic power and certainty. The blues in the *Lake of Brienz* have slightly faded, but the rich sombre harmony of the drawing is in no way impaired.

Another powerful and impressive drawing is the *Lake of Thun*. This differs in some important respects from the design engraved and published in the "Liber Studiorum."

An altogether different note is struck in the graceful and charming subject of *Bonneville*. Here all is peace and serenity. The foreground is filled with the amenities of untroubled rural life, the distant blue and white peaks of the mountains making an excellent foil to the graceful foliage, white walls and bridge of the little town which nestles at their feet. The foreground, indeed, is only redeemed from insipidity by the sharp, firm drawing of the ripples and stones.

THE RHINE DRAWINGS.

25. Mayence and Kastel. $8^{11}/_{16}$" × $14^{5}/_{8}$". (Plate XVIII.)

26. Mayence. $7^{3}/_{4}$" × $12^{1}/_{8}$". (Christie's, 1890.)

27. Mayence. $8^{3}/_{4}$" × $13^{7}/_{8}$". (Christie's, 1890; Taylor Sale, July 1912.)

28. Palace of Biebrich. 8" × $13^{1}/_{2}$". (Christie's, 1890; Turner House, Penarth.)

29. Johannisberg. $8^{13}/_{14}$" × $13^{1}/_{2}$". (Plate XXIII.)

30. Rüdesheim, looking to Bingen Klopp. $8^{1}/_{4}$" × $13^{1}/_{2}$". (Christie's, 1890.)

31. Bingen and Ehrenfels, from the Lake. $7^{5}/_{8}$" × $12^{1}/_{4}$".

32. Abbey of Bingen, looking towards Lake. 8" × 11½". (Plate XXV.)

33. The Mausethurm, Bingen Loch. 8" × 12¼".

34. Bausenberg in the Brohlthal. 8⅝" × 12¼". (Christie's, 1890.)

35. Sooneck, with Bacharach in the distance. $8^{15}/_{18}$" × 14½". (Plate XXI.)

36. Fürstenberg. 9¼" × 12¼". (Christie's, 1890.)

37. Bacharach and Stahleck. 7¾" × 12½". (Christie's, 1890.)

38. Pfalz, Caub and Gutenfels. 7¾" × 12⅛". (Christie's, 1890; Sir R. Hardy, Bart.)

39. Oberwesel and Schönburg Castle. 8⅝" × 14". (Christie's, 1890.)

40. Lurleiberg. $7^{13}/_{14}$" × 12⅛".

41. St. Goarshausen and Katz Castle. 7⅝" × 12". (Christie's, 1890; G. R. Burnett, Esq.)

42. Lurleiberg. 8" × 12".

43. Lurleiberg and St. Goarshausen. 8" × 12¼".

44. Lurleiberg. 7½" × 11¾". (Christie's, 1890; Lord Penrhyn.)

45. Lurleiberg. 7¾" × 12".

46. St. Goarshausen. 7⅞" × 12".

47. Lurleiberg. 7½" × 11¼". (Christie's, 1890; Louis Huth.)

48. Lurleiberg. 7½" × 11⅞". (Christie's, 1890; Sir H. Boulton.)

49. Katz Castle, with Rheinfels. 7½" × 12⅛". (Christie's, 1890.)

50. From Rheinfels, looking over St. Goar to Katz. 7⅞" × 12⅜". (Plate XXIX.)

51. Hirzenach. 8⅜" × 12½". (Plate XV.)

52. Rheinfels, looking to Katz and St. Goarshausen. 7½" × 12⅛". (Christie's, 1890.)

53. Castles of the Two Brothers, Sterrenberg and Liebenstein. 8⅛" × 12". (Christie's, 1890; J. F. Schwann, Esq.)

54. Boppard. 7⅜" × 12¼". (Christie's, 1890.)

55. Peterspay. 8¼" × 12½". (Christie's, 1890.)

56. Marksburg. 7⅝" × 12⅜". (Christie's, 1890.)

57. Oberlahnstein. 7⅝" × 12¼". (Christie's, 1890.)

58. Entrance of the Lahn. 7¾" × 12¼". (Christie's, 1890; Lord Penrhyn.)

59. Abbey near Coblenz. 7¾" × 8⅜".

60. The Back of Ehrenbreitstein, from the Pfaffen. 7¾" × 12¼". (Christie's, 1890.)

61. From Ehrenbreitstein. 7¾" × 12¼". (Christie's, 1890.)

62. Quay at Coblenz. 7¾" × 12¼". (Christie's, 1890.)

63. Bridge over the Moselle, Coblenz. 7⅝" x 12¼". (Christie's, 1890; Rev. W. Macgregor.)

64. Neuweid and Weissenthurm. 7¾" × 12¼". (Christie's, 1890; Agnew's Gallery, 1901.)

65. Weissenthurm, with Hoche's Monument. 7⅞" × 12½".

66. Andernach. 7¾" × 12¼". (Christie's, 1890.)

67. Roman Tower, Andernach. 7¾" × 12¼". (Christie's, 1890.)

68. Hammerstein. 7⅝" × 12⅜". (Christie's, 1890.)

69. Remagen and Linz. 7¾" × 12⅜". (Christie's, 1890; Sir J. Gibson Carmichael, Bart.)

70. Rolandswerth Nunnery and Drachenfels. 7¾" × 12⅛". (Christie's, 1890; Sir Donald Currie.)

71. Drachenfels and Nunnery. 9⅛" × 11⅜". (Christie's, 1890.)

72. Drachenfels. 9¼" × 11¼".

73. Godesberg. 7¾" × 11⅞". (Christie's, 1890.)

74. RhineGate, Cologne. 7¾" × 12". (Christie's, 1890.)

75. Cologne. 7¾" × 12". (Christie's, 1890.)

Details of the circumstances under which these fifty-one drawings were produced have been already given. No man, not even Turner, could possibly have sketched and worked up these subjects in the short space of a fortnight. But to have made even the sketches for this series of drawings in the short space of time Turner had at his disposal proves the marvellous rapidity with which he worked.

The drawings themselves are full of picturesque detail and accurate observation, but they are, perhaps, more remarkable for their technical skill than for their subject-matter. The deadly sureness of touch and almost incredible dexterity in the manipulation of washes of colour, remind one more of the calligraphic art of the Chinese and Japanese than of the work of an English landscape painter. If the early Swiss drawings in this collection may be described as an aftermath of Turner's romantic period, the Rhine drawings may be said to be the first instalment of the treasures of art which the great magician was to give us in the series of drawings of the Seine and Loire, and the later sketches of the Rhine and Moselle.

Though nearly three-quarters of this series were sold in 1890, the sixteen best drawings were carefully retained.

YORKSHIRE, MARINE, AND OTHER SUBJECTS.

76. Scarborough Town and Castle: Morning. Boys collecting Crabs. Exhibited R.A. 1811. 27" × 40". (Plate IV.)

77. Flounder Fishing, Putney Bridge. Exhibited R.A. 1811, under title November—Flounder Fishing. 24½" × 18½".

78. Cottage Steps; Children feeding Chickens. Exhibited R.A. 1811, under title May—Chickens. 24½" × 18½".

79. The Strid, Bolton Woods. 11¼" × 15½". (Plate VI.)

80. Bolton Abbey, from the South. Signed "J. M. W. Turner, R.A." 11¼" × 15½". (Plate XIII.)

81. Lancaster Sands. Signed "J. M. W. Turner, R.A., p.p." 11⅛" × 15½".

82. Man-of-War making Signals off the Mouth of the Tagus. 11" × 15½".

83. Wreck of an East Indiaman. 11¼" × 15¾".

84. Coniston Lake and Old Man. 19½" × 25½". (Plate X.)

85. Fish Market on the English Coast. Signed and dated "J. M. W. Turner, R.A., p.p., 1818." 11" × 15⅜". (Plate XXVIII.)

86. A First-Rater taking in Stores. Signed and dated "J. M. W. Turner, 1818." 11¼" × 15½". (Plate VIII.)

87. Loch Fyne. Signed and dated "J. M. W. Turner, R.A., 1810." 11" × 15½". (Christie's, 1890; Sir Donald Currie.)

88. Windermere. Signed and dated "J. M. W. Turner, R.A., 1821." 11½" × 16". (Christie's, 1890; Sir Donald Currie.)

89. Ulleswater. 11" × 15½". (Christie's, 1890.)

90. High Force: Fall of the Tees. 11" × 15½". (Christie's, 1890; Sir H. Doulton.)

91. Fountains Abbey. 11" × 15½". (Christie's, 1890; J. E. Taylor, Esq.)

THE WHARFEDALE SERIES.

92. Shooting Party on Hawksworth Moor, $11^{1}/_{16}$" × 15¾".

93. Hawksworth Hall. 11⅛" × 15½".

94. Otley, from the Chevin. 11" × 15½". (Plate XXII.)

95. Otley Bridge. 13½" × 17¾".

96. Caley Hall. 12" × 17½".

97. Old Dairy, Farnley. 12½" × 17¼".

98. Turner's Lodge. 12" × 16¾".

99. Stained Glass Window, 1819. 11½" × 12½".

100. Conservatory, Farnley Hall. 13¼" × 16½".

101. Lindley Hall. $11^{3}/_{16}$" × 15⅞".

102. Dining-Room, Farnley Hall. 12¼" × 17".

103. Entrance to the Gardens, Farnley. 12" × 16½".

104. Drawing-Room, Farnley Hall. 12¾" × 16½".

105. Front Staircase, Farnley Hall. 13" × 16¾".

106. The Banks of the Washburne. 13¼" × 16¼". (Plate XI.)

107. Lindley Bottom. 13½" × 17⅞".

108. Junction of Wharfe and Washburne. 12¼" x 17½".

109. The Library, Farnley Hall; facing fireplace. 13" × 17".

110. The Library, Farnley Hall; facing window. 12¼" × 16½".

111. Lindley Bridge and Hall. 12" × 17½". (Plate XXIV.)

112. Oak Staircase, Farnley Hall. 12½" × 16½".

113. Lindley Hall, from Lake Tiny. 11⅛" × $15^{7}/_{16}$".

114. Newall Old Hall. 12½" × 16½".

115. Oak Room, Farnley Hall. 11½" × 16".

116. Caley Park: Otley Chevin: Figures and dogs in foreground. 13½" × 17½".

117. The Washburne, with Leathley Church. 12" × 16¾". (Plate XVII.)

118. Caley Park, with Deer. 13½" × 17¾".

119. The Valley of the Wharfe, from Caley Park. 11¾" × 17½". (Plate II.)

120. Lake Tiny, Farnley, with boat and water-fowl in foreground. 11" × 15".

121. Wharfe, from Farnley Hall. 11¾" × 16½".

122. Lake Plantation, Farnley. 11³/₁₆" × 15½".

123. Lake Tiny, Farnley, with Almias Cliff in distance. 13½" × 17". (Plate XXX.)

124. Doorway, Farnley Hall. 10¾" × 12¾".

125. Farnley Hall and Garden, with Sun Dial. 12½" × 16¼".

126. The Carriage Drive, Farnley. 11¾" × 16". (Plate XXVII.)

127. Farnley in the Old Time. 11¼" × 15⅞".

128. View of Farnley Hall. 12¼" × 15½".

129. The Fairfax Cabinet. 11½" × 14½".

130. The Valley of the Washburne, and Lindley Bridge. 10¾" × 15½". (Christie's, 1890; Col. L. G. Fawkes.) (Plate XIX.)

131. In Wharfedale, with Temple, and Ducks in a pond. 13" × 17½". (Christie's, 1890.)

132. In Wharfedale, with rustic bridge. 11¼" x 15½". (Christie's, 1890.)

133. View of Otley Mills, with the River Wharfe and Mill Weir. (Christie's, 1890.)

134. The Pheasant's Nest, Farnley Park. 12" × 16¼". (Ruskin Collection.)

135. The Wood Walk, Farnley. 11" × 16¾". (F. Stevenson, Esq.)

136. Arthington Mill, near Farnley Hall. 10¾" x 15¼". (Taylor Sale, July 1912.)

137. Drawing-Room in 45, Grosvenor Place.

138. Frontispiece for Catalogue of Water-Colour Drawings in 45, Grosvenor Place.

139. London, from the windows of 45, Grosvenor Place, when in the possession of Walter Fawkes, Esq. 9¾" × 15¼". (Christie's, 1890; Agnew.)

BIRDS.

140. Dead Grouse, hanging. 10" × 7½".

141. Dead Grouse, hanging (Replica). 10¼" × 8¾". (Taylor Sale, 1912.)

142. Dead Wood Pigeon, 7" × 11".

143. Dead Blackcock. 10¼" × 9". (Taylor Sale, 1912.)

144. Head of Partridge. 3½" × 3½".

145. Head of Moor Game. 3½" × 4".

146. Head of Green Woodpecker. 5" × 5½".

147. Head of Guinea Fowl. 3½" × 3½".

148. Head of Moor Hawk. 3½" × 5".

149. Head of Woodcock. 4" × 6".

150. Head of White Owl. 7" × 7".

151. The Redbreast. 4½" × 6".

152. The Jay. 6" × 8¾".

153. Head of Heron, fish in mouth. 9" × 11".

154. Head of Peacock. 11" × 7".

155. The Goldfinch. 6" × 5".

156. Head of Game-Cock. 7" × 8¼".

157. Dead Kingfisher. 5½" × 5".

158. Head of Cuckoo. 2½" × 2¾".

159. Head of Hen Pheasant. 4" × 3¾".

160. Head of Cock Pheasant. 4¼" × 4¼".

161. Head of Turkey. 4½" × 4½".

VIGNETTES, &c.

162. Pedigree.

163. Frontispiece to Poets. "Three Poets in three different Kingdoms born." $7^9/_{16}$" × $5^9/_{16}$".

164. Greek Scene: "'Tis Greece, but living Greece no more."—Byron's *Giaour*. 7½" × 5½".

165. Norham Castle, 7½" × 5½". (Plate XXVI.)

166. Melrose: Moonlight. $7^{11}/_{16}$" × 5¼".

167. Glenartney:

"Here, 'twixt rock and river, grew
A dismal grove of sable hue."
Scott's *Rokeby*. $7^{13}/_{16}$" × 5½".

168. Lalla Rookh. 7½" × 5½".

169. Pyramids. Frontispiece to Ancient History.

170. Stonehenge. Frontispiece to Modern History.

171. Top of Snuff-box—Grouse, Partridge and Gun.

172. Edward I. The Stone of Scone. 12¼" × 9".

173. A gold coin found at Agincourt. Presented to Walter Fawkes, Esq., by Maj.-Gen. Sir Edward Barnes, 1823. 12¼" × 9½".

174. Reformation. 13" × 8¼".

175. Charles I. 9" × 6¾".

176. Banners of the Parliamentarians. 8¼" × 6⅝".

177. First Period. 11½" × 7¾".

178. Second Period. 11½" × 7¾".

179. Third Period. 12" × 8¼".

180. Fourth Period. 12¼" × 8¼".

181. Oliver Cromwell. 11½" × 8¼".

182. Richard Cromwell. 12" × 8¼".

183. Revolution, 1688. 7¾" × 6½".

184. Fairfaxiana. 9½" × 6".

185. Fairfax's Chair, Sword and Mace. 8½" × 6½".

186. Fairfax's Helmet, Sword and Drum. 11½" × 7½".

187. Fairfax's Cabinet. 11" × 14".

188. Cause and Effect. 11½" × 7½".

ITALIAN AND LATER SWISS DRAWINGS.

189. The Rialto, Venice. 11¼" × 16⅜". (Plate XX.)

190. The Colosseum, Rome. Inscribed and signed "Colliceum, Rome, J. M. W. Turner, 1820." 11" × 15½". (Plate XIV.)

191. Interior of St. Peter's, Rome. Signed and dated "J. M. W. Turner, 1820." 11½" × 16½". (Plate V.)

192. Upper Falls of the Reichenbach: Rainbow. 11⅛" × 15¾". (Plate XVI.)

193. The Passage of Mont Cenis. Signed "J. M. W. Turner," and inscribed "Passage of Mt. Cenis, Jan. 15, 1820." 11¼" × 15¾". (Plate VII.)

194. Rome, from Monte Mario. 11" × 15½". (Christie's, 1890; Sir Donald Currie.)

195. Rome, from the Pincian Hill. 11" × 15½". (Christie's, 1890; Sir Donald Currie.)

196. Mount Vesuvius in Eruption. 11" × 15½". (Christie's, 1890; W. Newall, Esq.)

197. Naples. 11" × 15½". (Christie's, 1890.)

198. Venice, from Fusina. 11¼" × 15½". (Christie's, 1890; Sir Donald Currie.)

CONCLUSION.

There can be no doubt that the money spent by Mr. Walter Fawkes upon Turner's drawings and paintings was well expended. Regarded merely as an investment, it was extremely profitable. The drawing of *Mont Blanc, from the Val d'Aosta* (24), for which Mr. Fawkes paid fifty guineas, was sold for a thousand guineas in 1890; that of *Windermere* (88), which cost twenty-five guineas, was sold at the same time for twelve hundred guineas: and the auction price of Turner's work has doubled, and sometimes trebled, since 1890. Roughly speaking, Mr. Fawkes spent about three thousand pounds on the collection, and its market price to-day is certainly not less than a hundred and fifty thousand pounds.

But the real value of such a collection cannot be estimated in terms of pounds, shillings and pence. The influence exerted by these lovely records of Farnley Hall and the neighbouring country upon Mr. Fawkes's family and descendants has been more precious than gold. They have dignified and hallowed the ancestral home and lands, refined and educated the taste of all who have been privileged to live among them, and they have made the name of Walter Fawkes for ever memorable in the annals of British Art.

ALEXANDER J. FINBERG.

The Editor desires to acknowledge his indebtedness to Mr. F. H. Fawkes, the present owner of Farnley Hall, who has kindly placed at his disposal the beautiful drawings by Turner reproduced in this work.

BONNEVILLE, SAVOY.

CIRCA 1808. SIZE 11" × 15⅜".

The "Liber Studiorum" plate (R. 64), published January 1, 1816, was founded on this design. The plate, which was engraved from a sepia drawing, shows several slight variations from the water-colour; the buildings in the centre and the bridge on the right are heightened, the stick leaning on the blue and white bundle in the foreground has been omitted, the hat of the girl resting on a stone on the left has been taken off, the figure of a boy added, and a group of sheep substituted for the herd of goats in the centre.

THE VALLEY OF THE WHARFE, FROM CALEY PARK.

CIRCA 1816-1818. SIZE 11¾" × 17½".

This drawing is executed in body-colour on brown paper. It represents one of the views in the neighbourhood of Farnley Hall. The River Wharfe winds through the valley in the middle distance. On the left, the junction with the Washburne is shown; on the right, in the distance, is Poole Bridge. Above the junction of the Wharfe and the Washburne, Leathley Church and village are seen, and beyond them the gaunt shoulders of Great Alms Cliff appear above the horizon.

THE VALLEY OF CHAMOUNIX.

SIGNED AND DATED "J. M. W. TURNER, R.A., P.P., 1809 (?)" SIZE 11¼' × 15⅝".

Made from sketches executed during Turner's first visit to Switzerland in 1802. The snow-capped mountains in the distance no doubt belong to the chain of Mont Blanc.

SCARBOROUGH TOWN AND CASTLE: MORNING. BOYS COLLECTING CRABS.

CIRCA 1809. SIZE 27" × 40".

Turner exhibited a drawing with this title at the Royal Academy, 1811, but it is uncertain whether it was this drawing or the one now in the Wallace Collection. The latter is signed and dated "J. M. W. Turner, R.A., 1809."

INTERIOR OF ST. PETER'S, ROME.

SIGNED AND DATED "J. M. W. TURNER, 1820." SIZE 11½" × 16½".

One of Turner's first Italian drawings from his own sketches, the illustrations to Hakewill's "Italy" having been made before Turner visited Italy, from camera obscura tracings made by Hakewill.

THE STRID, BOLTON WOODS.

CIRCA 1811. SIZE 11¼" × 15½".

The pencil-drawing on which this is based is in the National Gallery ("Farnley and related subjects," CLIV, U.). A beautifully balanced and complete design, without any sacrifice of local truth.

THE PASSAGE OF MONT CENIS.

SIGNED "J. M. W. TURNER" AND INSCRIBED "PASSAGE OF MT. CENIS, JAN. 15, 1820."

SIZE 11¼" × 15¾".

An incident Turner witnessed on his return from his first visit to Italy. The snow made it difficult to cross the Alps at that time of the year. His sketch-book, "Return from Italy" (CXCII), is full of rough pencil-sketches of the snow and storm effects. Among some hasty scribbles on one page appear the following memoranda:—"Men shovelling away snow from the carriage—Women and children hugging(?)—The sky pink—The light and the cast shadows rather warm—Trees are all covered with the snow—The trees in the distance and wood getting darker." This is one of the most beautiful and impressive of the Farnley drawings.

A FIRST-RATER TAKING IN STORES.

SIGNED AND DATED "J. M. W. TURNER, 1818." SIZE 11¼" × 15½".

This is the drawing Turner is said to have begun and finished one morning at Farnley, between breakfast and lunch. There had been some talk at breakfast between Mr. Fawkes and Turner about the relative sizes of small sailing-craft and men-of-war. After breakfast, Turner said to young Hawksworth Fawkes that he would make a drawing to illustrate what they had been talking about. The boy sat beside him for three hours while the drawing was being made, the artist, says Thornbury, "tearing up the sea with the eagle-claw of his thumbnail, and working like a madman; yet the detail is full and delicate, betraying no sign of hurry." This story has been frequently repeated, but it is hard, with the exquisitely finished and elaborate drawing in front of one, to accept it without considerable reservation.

THE GREAT FALL OF THE REICHENBACH; IN THE VALLEY OF HASLE, SWITZERLAND.

SIGNED AND DATED "J. M. W. TURNER, R.A., 1804." SIZE 40" × 27".

Painted from sketches made in 1802. Exhibited at the Royal Academy, 1815, under the above title, together with two other Farnley drawings, viz., *The Passage of Mount St. Gothard* and *Lake of Lucerne*.

CONISTON LAKE AND OLD MAN.

CIRCA 1816-1818. SIZE 19½" × 25½".

This drawing is executed in body-colour on brown paper. Mr. Ruskin's house and grounds stand not far from the spot from which it was made.

THE BANKS OF THE WASHBURNE.

CIRCA 1818. SIZE 13¼" × 16¼".

This drawing is executed in body-colour on brown paper. It shows a bend of the Washburne about a mile from Farnley Hall. Leathley Church stands a little to the left, just out of the picture. In the distance is seen the rocky crest of the Otley Chevin, with Caley Park on the slopes below. The banks are now covered with a dense growth of trees, entirely obliterating the view of the river. This drawing is based on a small pencil-sketch in the "Hastings" sketch-book (CXXXIX, pp. 35a & 36).

THE LAKE OF BRIENZ—MOONLIGHT.

SIGNED "J. M. W. TURNER, R.A." CIRCA 1804. SIZE 11" × 15½".

The pencil-sketch of this view, made in Switzerland in 1802, is in the National Gallery (LXXVII, p. 34). It has an "F" written in ink in the corner, evidently put there when Mr. Fawkes ordered this drawing. There is also a colour-study in the same collection (LXXX, E.). The blue has slightly faded in this drawing, but the general effect remains harmonious and very impressive.

BOLTON ABBEY, FROM THE SOUTH.

CIRCA 1812. SIGNED "J. M. W. TURNER, R.A." SIZE 11¼" × 15½".

There are a number of pencil-drawings of Bolton Abbey in the "Devonshire Rivers, No. 3, and Wharfedale" sketch-book (cxxxiv). The water-mark of this sketch-book is 1811, so the date of the sketches may be a year or two later.

THE COLOSSEUM, ROME.

INSCRIBED AND SIGNED "COLLICEUM, ROME, J. M. W. TURNER, 1820." SIZE 11" × 15½".

Based on the pencil-drawing ("Rome: C. Studies," CLXXXIX, p. 23) made in Rome in 1819.

HIRZENACH.

DATE 1817. SIZE 8⅜" × 12½".

One of the Rhine series. This drawing is executed in water-colour on white paper, but a grey preparation was washed over the paper before the painting was commenced.

Hirzenach is near St. Goar, where Turner is known to have been on the 23rd, 24th and 27th of August, 1817. There are sketches of Hirzenach and the neighbourhood in the "Waterloo and Rhine" sketch-book (CXL).

UPPER FALLS OF THE REICHENBACH: RAINBOW.

CIRCA 1818. SIZE 11⅛" × 15¾".

The white line of the falls is seen on the left in shadow, contrasting with the warm sunlight on the rock in the centre of design. The rainbow on the right is formed by the spray of the falls. In foreground, on left, just below the falls, are a peasant girl and dog (the white dress of the girl and the white dog are dug out with the penknife). An exquisitely delicate drawing, full of subtleties of form and colour.

THE WASHBURNE, WITH LEATHLEY CHURCH.
CIRCA 1818. SIZE 12" × 16¾".

This drawing is executed in body-colour on brown paper. The River Washburne, with water-mill, is seen in the foreground, Leathley Church on the hill in the middle-distance, and the Otley Chevin, with Caley Park, beyond. The steep wooded bank on the right of the river in the middle-distance is the scene of the drawing *The Banks of the Washburne* (Plate XI). The drawing of *The Valley of the Washburne, and Lindley Bridge* (Plate XIX) was made from a spot near the mill in the foreground, looking towards the right.

MAYENCE AND KASTEL.

DATE 1817. SIZE $8^{11}/_{16}$" × $14^{5}/_{8}$".

One of the Rhine drawings. The dark cloud in the centre is an instance of Turner's wonderful technical daring and resource, the effect being obtained by the use of wet, running colour. Turner was at Mayence on 24th and 25th August, 1817.

THE VALLEY OF THE WASHBURNE, AND LINDLEY BRIDGE.

CIRCA 1818. SIZE $10^{3}/_{4}$" × $15^{1}/_{2}$".

A view of the Washburne looking north towards Stainburn, taken from a spot near the water-mill shown in the foreground of *The Washburne, with*

Leathley Church (Plate XVII). Lindley Hall appears on the eminence to the right. This drawing is now in the possession of Colonel Lionel G. Fawkes.

THE RIALTO, VENICE.

CIRCA 1820. SIZE 11¼" × 16⅜".

This drawing is frequently mistaken for the original of the engraving of the same subject published in Hakewill's "Italy" (Rawlinson's "Engraved Work of J. M. W. Turner," p. 80), but the differences between the drawing and the engraving are too marked and extensive for this to be possible. The Hakewill drawing was made before Turner visited Venice, from camera obscura sketches by Hakewill. The Farnley drawing was made immediately after Turner's return from Italy in 1820, from his own sketches. It is interesting as being Turner's first Venetian picture.

SOONECK, WITH BACHARACH IN THE DISTANCE.

DATE 1817. SIZE 8$^{15}/_{16}$" × 14½".

The slender tower of Sooneck, commanding the entrance to a ravine, stands on the left; beyond it, in shadow, rise the ruins of Fürstenberg. Opposite the Fürstenberg, on the right bank of the Wisper, which fells into the Rhine here, stands the ruined castle of Nollich. The rugged cliff on this side of the Rhine is called the "Devil's Ladder."

OTLEY, FROM THE CHEVIN.

CIRCA 1818. SIZE 11" × 15½".

From the deer park on the Otley Chevin we look down on the houses and church of Otley, the "metropolis of Wharfedale," as its inhabitants call it. Beyond, the Wharfe winds away towards Ilkley and Bolton, and on the left may be seen the Cow and Calf Rocks at Ben Rhydding.

This is one of the most poetical and exquisitely finished drawings of the Wharfedale series.

JOHANNISBERG.

DATE 1817. SIZE $8^{15}/_{16}$" × $13\frac{1}{2}$".

Schloss Johannisberg stands on a vine-clad eminence in the centre of the drawing; and on the bank, a little to the right, is seen Winkel.

LINDLEY BRIDGE AND HALL.

CIRCA 1818. SIZE 12" × 17½".

A nearer view of Lindley Bridge than that in Plate XIX. The Lindley Wood Reservoir has now been formed just above the bridge.

ABBEY OF BINGEN, LOOKING TOWARDS LAKE.

DATE 1817. SIZE 8" × 11½".

The ruins of the old collegiate church are seen on the right, and beyond, the "Bridge of Drusus," crossing the River Nahe.

NORHAM CASTLE.

CIRCA 1823. SIZE 7½" × 5⅝".

One of the illustrations to the "Three Poets in three different Kingdoms born," viz., Scott, Byron, and Moore.

THE CARRIAGE DRIVE, FARNLEY.

CIRCA 1818. SIZE 11¾" × 16".

The two oaks in the foreground, with fragments of their seats, are still to be found half-way up the carriage drive; but the trees round them have grown so that they shut out the distant view of the river and Otley Bridge. Otley Church appears in the middle distance on the left in the drawing.

FISH MARKET ON THE ENGLISH COAST.

SIGNED AND DATED "J. M. W. TURNER, R.A., P.P., 1818." SIZE 11" × 15⅜".

A slightly different version in oils of this design, known as *Fish Market at Hastings*, was painted some years earlier for Mr. Jack Fuller. It was sold at Christie's recently in the Acland-Hood sale.

FROM RHEINFELS, LOOKING OVER ST. GOAR TO KATZ.

DATE 1817. SIZE 7⅞" × 12⅜".

The town of St. Goar lies stretched out at our feet. Across the river are seen St. Goarshausen and the ruined castle of the Cat (Katz), half-way up the hill above it. A curious morning effect, before the sun has dispelled the vapours rising from the river.

LAKE TINY, FARNLEY, WITH ALMIAS CLIFF IN DISTANCE.

CIRCA 1818. SIZE 13½" × 17".

View looking north-east from Farnley Park. Almias Cliff is just visible in the distance on the left. On the right appears the group of trees on the slope of the hill just above Leathley Church.

Milton Keynes UK
Ingram Content Group UK Ltd.
UKHW042146281024
450365UK00010B/663